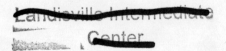

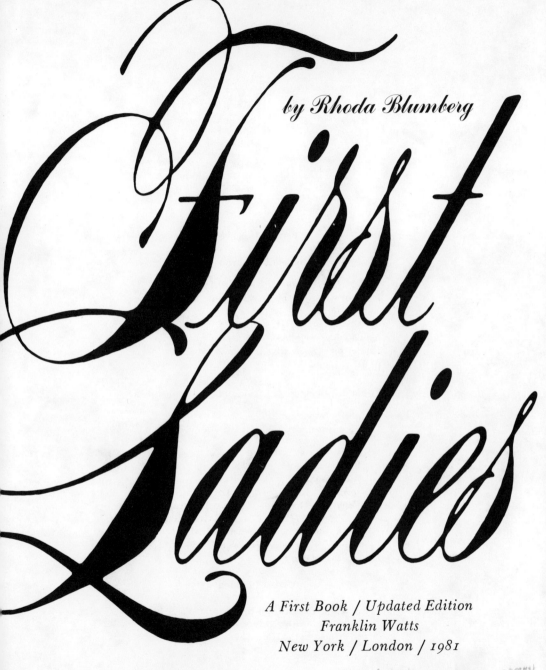

by Rhoda Blumberg

First Ladies

A First Book / Updated Edition
Franklin Watts
New York / London / 1981

Cover by Beehive Design Studio, Inc.

Photographs courtesy of:

The Mount Vernon Ladies' Association: p. 2; Library of Congress: pp. 4, 6, 8, 9, 10, 11, 12, 13, 14, 15, 17, 18, 19, 20, 22, 23, 25, 27, 28, 29, 31, 32, 33, 34, 36, 37, 39, 41, 43, 45, 47, 49, 51, 55; The Lyndon Baines Johnson Library: p. 53; The White House: pp. 57, 59; United Press International, Inc.: p. 61.

Library of Congress Cataloging in Publication Data

Blumberg, Rhoda.
　　First ladies

　　(A First book)
　　Bibliography: p.
　　Includes index.
　　SUMMARY: Brief biographies of the women who have been First Ladies of the United States.
　　　1. Presidents—United States—Wives—Biography —Juvenile literature. [1. First Ladies] I. Title.
E176.2.B58　　973'.0992 [B] [920]　　　77-2617
ISBN 0-531-01286-7

Updated Edition

Contents

For my delightful daughter, Alice

Introduction

"What American woman wouldn't want her husband to be President?" Mamie Eisenhower asked. Dolley Madison loved every minute in the White House; Rachel Jackson didn't want to live in "that palace." Julia Grant declared that being First Lady was "the happiest period" in her life; Jackie Kennedy said she felt like "a piece of public property."

Some First Ladies were brilliant; others were dull. Some loved being in the public eye; others suffered when people criticized them. Some were ignored because they didn't seem glamorous or interesting. Others were distressed because reporters followed them and they had no privacy.

Although most First Ladies limited their duties to household matters and entertaining, some influenced history as advisers to their husbands. One woman was not only a chief adviser, but also a capable "President" during her husband's long illness.

The Constitution has nothing to say about the duties of a First Lady. She is not "sworn in," but she is expected to be an active, gracious hostess for the President.

Today First Ladies don't confine themselves to being hostesses. They campaign, give press interviews, and talk about important issues over radio and television.

Martha Dandridge Custis Washington

1731–1802

Born: New Kent County, Virginia
Married: Daniel Parke Custis, 1749; widowed 1757
Children: Jack, Patsy, and two infants who died

Married: George Washington, 1759
Children: None
First Lady: 1789–1797

Martha Washington worried about becoming First Lady. What was expected of her? How was she to act? Would the President set up a formal court for the new nation? Martha was a tired fifty-eight-year-old grandmother who wrote that "younger and gayer women" would make the best First Ladies.

The "President's Palace" was a small, three-story brick house in a poor section of New York City. Martha was relieved to learn that a staff planned the social events. The President would host Tuesday afternoon receptions, called "levees," for men only. Martha would be hostess at Thursday dinners and at Friday night tea parties. The dinners were stiff and formal. The tea parties were enjoyable for most, but dull for Martha, who remained seated throughout the evening. Servants announced guests who greeted "Lady Washington" first, then wandered off to see the President and chat with friends. Martha saw to it that guests departed at nine o'clock, the President's bedtime.

Martha's manner was friendly and warm. She was one of our best-loved First Ladies.

Like most women of her time, she was trained to be a housewife. Although brought up in comfort, she had never been to school. At seventeen Martha married Daniel Parke Custis, a wealthy man more than twice her age. He died eight years later.

Friends introduced the widow to Colonel George Washington, who married her and made her mistress of Mount Vernon. Though they had no children of their own, George adopted Jack and Patsy, Martha's children from her first marriage. Unfortunately, Patsy died at the age of seventeen, and Jack died when he was twenty-six. The Washingtons adopted two of Jack's children, George and Nellie. They became part of the President's household.

The first year Martha was First Lady she wrote, "I think I am more like a state prisoner than anything else." When Washington's term ended and they returned to Mount Vernon, she said they both felt "like children just released from school."

Abigail Smith Adams

1744–1818

Born: Weymouth, Massachusetts
Married: John Adams, 1764
Children: John Quincy, Thomas, Charles,
Abigail, Susanna (died as infant)
First Lady: 1797–1801

Living at a time when a woman was not supposed to express important opinions, Abigail Adams refused to "hold her tongue." She believed women deserved to vote and have an education equal to that of men. She also opposed slavery.

Reporters, complaining that a female was using her influence on the President, called Abigail "Her Majesty" and "Mrs. President."

In 1800 the Adams moved from the presidential home in Philadelphia to the White House, an unfinished building in the middle of the ugly, muddy town of Washington. Only six rooms were livable. Abigail hung her laundry in the now-famous East Room.

Abigail Adams was the only wife of a President whose son, John Quincy Adams, also became President.

Martha Wayles Skelton Jefferson

1748–1782

Born: Charles City County, Virginia
Married: Bathurst Skelton, 1766; widowed 1768
Children: John

Married: Thomas Jefferson, 1772
Children: Patsy, Jane, a son who died in infancy,
Mary, Lucy, Lucy Elizabeth

Martha Jefferson died almost nineteen years before her husband became President. When she died Jefferson swore he would never remarry; no one could replace the wife he loved. No portrait of her exists.

During their ten-year marriage four of their six children died. Only two daughters, Patsy and Mary, lived to see their father become President.

Jefferson did not want anyone to act as First Lady. On occasion he asked his friend Dolley Madison to be hostess. She was the wife of his Secretary of State. Jefferson's married daughter, Patsy, also acted as hostess.

Dolley Payne Todd Madison

1768–1849

Born: Guilford County, North Carolina
Married: John Todd, 1790; widowed 1793
Children: John Payne, William (died in infancy)

Married: James Madison, 1794
Children: None
First Lady: 1809–1817

When James Madison became President the capital enjoyed an explosion of lavish parties, starring a charming, gorgeously gowned First Lady. Dolley Madison became world-famous as a hostess. Her gaiety and warmth impressed statesmen and servants. Dolley had a rare memory for names and faces, and she made everyone feel important. She was a charmer.

Although plump, middle-aged, and no great beauty, she was a model many American women imitated. Newspapers were interested in everything Dolley wore: her jewelry, headdresses, and her expensive Parisian gowns. Because she carried a snuff box, it became common for Washington women to take snuff. Card playing, wearing rouge and feathered turbans were "in" because of Dolley.

It is hard to believe that a quiet Quaker girl from a small village became one of our most famous hostesses. Dolley had little education, except for religious instruction. She was poor until she married John Todd, a successful lawyer. He died of yellow fever three years later, leaving Dolley with two small children.

Madison met Dolley when he was forty-three and she was twenty-six. He was an unattractive, scholarly, dull little man, but Dolley loved him. He became her "darling little husband."

When the United States was at war with England from 1812 to 1814, Dolley gave parties that kept up everyone's spirits. She was forced to cancel a dinner the day before the British invaded Washington on August 24, 1814. Dolley heard cannons, and saw soldiers in the streets, but she remained in the White House long enough to save the original draft of the Constitution and the Declaration of Independence, packing them in her trunk. She saved Stuart's famous portrait of Washington by removing it from its frame and handing it to people fleeing to New York. The British were burning public buildings as she left, and they set fire to the White House shortly after her departure.

When the Madisons returned a few days later, only charred walls remained of the White House. Dolley wrote she would have been willing to brave the Redcoats and remain "if I could have had a cannon through every window" of the White House.

Elizabeth Kortright Monroe

1768–1830

Born: New York City
Married: James Monroe, 1786
Children: Eliza, Maria, Monroe (died as infant)
First Lady: 1817–1825

When Elizabeth Monroe became First Lady she was ailing and had little interest in parties. When she did appear at White House functions she looked beautiful, but was stiff, formal, and quiet. Elizabeth was accused of being a snob.

Washington society became furious when the Monroes' younger daughter, Maria, was married in the White House, and the wedding was so small that even Cabinet members were not invited.

The woman who offended so many as First Lady charmed Paris when her husband was minister to France before he became President.

Louisa Catherine Johnson Adams

1775–1852

Born: London, England
Married: John Quincy Adams, 1797
Children: George Washington, John,
Charles Francis, a girl who died in infancy
First Lady: 1825–1829

Louisa, the daughter of an American consul to England, was an American citizen born and brought up in Europe. John Quincy Adams met her when President Washington sent him on a diplomatic mission to London. They were married in 1797, the year John's father became President. John served as minister in Prussia, Russia, and England. Louisa enjoyed living in Berlin and London, but she suffered in Russia. The harsh winters made her ill, and an infant daughter died there.

When Adams became President Monroe's Secretary of State, Louisa became the capital's outstanding party-giver. Unfortunately, by the time she became First Lady she was too ill to continue charming the capital.

Rachel Donelson Robards Jackson

1767–1828

Born: Halifax County, Virginia
Married: Lewis Robards, 1785; divorced 1793
Children: None

Married: Andrew Jackson, 1791; remarried 1794
Children: None
First Lady: Died December 22, 1828, after Jackson
was elected but before he was inaugurated.

A Cincinnati newspaper said that Rachel was "not a suitable person to be placed at the head of the female society of the United States." Pamphlets were printed about Jackson stealing another man's wife and marrying a woman who was not divorced.

Jackson had, indeed, married Rachel, both of them believing her first husband had divorced her. But after their marriage they discovered her divorce was not final and they had to remarry. After enduring so much criticism, Rachel declared she did not wish to live in "that palace" in Washington.

Her wish came true. She died seven weeks after the election. Emily Donelson, the wife of one of their adopted sons, acted as Jackson's hostess.

Hannah Hoes Van Buren

1783–1819

Born: Kinderhook, New York
Married: Martin Van Buren, 1807
Children: Abraham, John, Martin, Jr., Smith Thompson
White House Hostess: Angelica Van Buren,
of South Carolina, wife of son, Abraham, 1838–1841

Martin Van Buren's wife, Hannah, died eighteen years before he was elected President. Little is known about her, for although Van Buren wrote an eight-hundred-page autobiography, he never mentioned his wife.

Van Buren's daughter-in-law, Angelica Singleton, acted as First Lady. Although all admired her beauty, many complained about her extravagances. She was accused of trying to make the White House look like a royal court. Elaborately dressed, she sat on a raised platform as she received guests, like a queen greeting subjects from a throne.

Van Buren was also accused of affecting airs. He and Angelica were quite a contrast to the plain, unpolished Jacksons.

Anna Tuthill Symmes Harrison

1775–1864

Born: Near Morristown, New Jersey
Married: William Henry Harrison, 1795
Children: Elizabeth, John, Lucy, William,
Benjamin, Mary, Carter, Anna, James, John Scott
First Lady: March 4–April 4, 1841

Anna Harrison never wanted her husband to be President. When she learned that he had won the election, she said, "I wish that my husband's friends had left him where he is, happy and contented in his retirement." Anna was sixty-five years old and ailing, too weak to travel to the inauguration.

She never saw the White House. Her husband died a month after he became President. Anna received the news of his death as she was packing to leave for the capital.

Anna endured a long, tragic life. Of the ten children she reared, only five survived long enough to see their father elected President. By the time she died, at the age of eighty-eight, only one of her children was alive.

Letitia Christian Tyler

1790–1842

Born: New Kent County, Virginia
Married: John Tyler, 1813
Children: Mary, Robert, John, Letitia, Elizabeth,
Anne (died in infancy), Alice, Tazewell
First Lady: 1841–1842

Letitia Tyler spent only one year of her life in the White House. She became paralyzed two years before her husband became President. Confined to a wheelchair, she remained out of sight, upstairs in the White House, and was brought down only once, for her daughter's wedding. She died in the White House.

Priscilla Tyler, a pretty daughter-in-law, took over the role of White House hostess.

Julia Gardiner Tyler

1820–1889

Born: Gardiner's Island, New York
Married: John Tyler, 1844
Children: David, John, Julia,
Lachlan, Lyon, Robert, Pearl
First Lady: 1844–1845

In 1843 a high-society New York glamour girl moved to Washington to meet the "right people." Julia Gardiner, twenty-three, gorgeous and charming, really swept men off their feet. Two congressmen and a Supreme Court justice are said to have been among the many who wanted to marry her. Julia was delighted to accept a President's proposal.

She was First Lady only eight months, but the White House hadn't sparkled so since the days of Dolley Madison. Sometimes Julia sat on a raised platform, expensively gowned, surrounded by white-robed maids of honor. She hired a press agent to make sure reporters wrote nice things about her.

Sarah Childress Polk

1803–1891

Born: Murfreesboro, Tennessee
Married: James Polk, 1824
Children: None
First Lady: 1845–1849

Believing that a First Lady's duty was to help and advise the President, Sarah Polk worked with her husband twelve hours a day. James Polk confided in her and listened to her views on state matters. Since it wasn't seemly for females to voice serious opinions, Sarah was careful to say "Mr. Polk believes . . ." before she discussed her political ideas with others.

Sarah Polk was not typical of her time, nor was her mother, who persuaded the headmaster of a boys' school to tutor her daughter. Then her mother sent Sarah away from their Tennessee plantation to one of the few good schools for girls, the Female Academy of Salem, North Carolina. She grew up to be a beautiful woman with a brain she knew how to use.

Margaret Mackall Smith Taylor

1788–1852

Born: Calvert County, Maryland
Married: Zachary Taylor, 1810
Children: Sarah, Richard, Betty,
Ann, Octavia, Margaret
First Lady: 1849–1850

After thirty years on isolated army posts, Margaret Taylor wanted to retire to a quiet life in a four-room cottage. Of the six children she reared, only three were alive when her husband became President. She was sixty years old, and her spirit was broken by sorrow.

Margaret so disliked moving to the White House that she declared she would never act as First Lady. She remained in her rooms upstairs, where she saw her old friends and it was rumored that she smoked her corncob pipe. Claiming poor health, she assigned the duties of hostess to her daughter Betty Taylor Bliss.

Zachary Taylor died sixteen months after he became President. Margaret died two years later, never speaking of her life as First Lady. No portrait of her exists.

Abigail Powers Fillmore

1798–1853

Born: Stillwater, New York
Married: Millard Fillmore, 1826
Children: Mary, Millard
First Lady: 1850–1853

Abigail was a poor girl from upstate New York whose father died when she was two years old. Her widowed mother took in boarders to eke out a living and to save enough to give Abigail an education in New Hope, New York. At school she met a poor boy who earned $55 a year as a clothmaker. The boy was Millard Fillmore. They were married six years after they met.

Abigail became a schoolteacher, one of the few professions open to women at that time. Fillmore became a lawyer, a congressman, Vice President, and President when President Taylor died.

Partly lame from an old ankle injury, Abigail was most comfortable in her room reading. She started the first library in the White House.

Jane Means Appleton Pierce

1806–1863

Born: Hampton, New Hampshire
Married: Franklin Pierce, 1834
Children: a son who died in infancy, Frank, Benny
First Lady: 1853–1857

When Jane Pierce learned that her husband had won the presidential nomination, she fainted. During his campaign she prayed he would lose the election. Jane believed Washington and politics were evil.

The Pierces suffered tragic lives. Two of their three young sons died. Their remaining child, eleven-year-old Benny, was killed before their eyes two months before the inauguration. A train in which they were riding jumped the tracks, fell over, and crushed out the boy's life.

Jane was convinced that Benny's death was the Lord's punishment for her husband's ambition to be President. Locking herself in her room, she would talk and write letters to her dead sons. She lived in a fantasy world with her dead children until she died at the age of fifty-seven.

Harriet Lane

1830–1903

Born: Franklin County, Pennsylvania
Niece of James Buchanan, bachelor President
First Lady: 1857–1861

Harriet Lane was First Lady for our only bachelor President, her uncle, James Buchanan, who served just before the outbreak of the Civil War. After she was orphaned at the age of eleven, Buchanan became her guardian. He sent her to the best schools and took her to London when he was ambassador to England.

Washington adored having a pretty young woman as First Lady, especially after the gloomy years of President Pierce. To be sure that her parties would be pleasant for all, Harriet asked her guests not to talk politics.

Five years after leaving the White House, Harriet married Henry Elliott Johnston, a wealthy banker. She amassed priceless paintings, which she willed to the government. They are at the National Gallery of Art in Washington.

Mary Todd Lincoln

1818–1882

Born: Lexington, Kentucky
Married: Abraham Lincoln, 1842
Children: Robert, Edward, Willie, Tad
First Lady: 1861–1865

Mary Lincoln was delighted to become First Lady of the Land. But her life was a nightmare.

On entering the White House she discovered that hundreds of letters had been sent threatening both Lincoln's life and her own. She had to live with fear.

Anxious to be an elegant First Lady, she bought expensive clothes at prices she could not afford. But those she tried to impress called her spending vulgar.

Because her family was from the South, and her brothers served in the Confederate Army, she was even accused of being a spy. Lincoln was called before a congressional committee to defend her loyalty.

In 1862 their twelve-year-old son, Willie, died. Eddie, another son, had died when he was four years old in 1850. The loss of a second child was almost too much for Mary to bear.

By the time Lincoln started his second term of office, she was half crazed. Because spending money always made her feel better, she paid $2,000 for her inaugural gown, and she bought three hundred pairs of lace gloves within four months.

Mary could not control her temper in public. Several times she flew into a jealous rage when Lincoln talked with another woman.

On April 14, 1865, while holding Mary's hand, Lincoln was assassinated. Six years later her youngest son, Tad, died at the age of eighteen. Thereafter Mary lost her sanity. She imagined she was penniless and about to be poisoned.

Mary was once a bright, attractive young woman from Lexington, Kentucky, who attended the finest finishing schools. While visiting a sister in Springfield, Illinois, she met Lincoln and married him. The girl who had been used to servants moved into rooms in rundown Globe Tavern, where Lincoln paid $4.00 a week for rent. She did not mind, for she adored her husband. Mary claimed she knew that he would become a great man.

Lincoln loved her dearly. Understanding her emotional weaknesses, he called her his "child-wife."

Eliza McCardle Johnson

1810–1876

Born: Leesburg, Tennessee
Married: Andrew Johnson, 1827
Children: Martha, Charles, Robert, Mary, Andrew, Jr.
First Lady: 1865–1869

Eliza's father was a shoemaker in Greeneville, Tennessee. He died when she was a little girl. Her mother managed to support herself and her daughter by making quilts and sandals. Eliza helped her mother after school.

Andrew Johnson, an eighteen-year-old tailor, came to Greeneville in a broken-down cart drawn by a half-blind pony and set up shop there. Within a year he and sixteen-year-old Eliza fell in love, married, and moved into the back of his shop. Andrew had never gone to school. Eliza taught him to read and write. When he sewed in his tailor shop she read books to him.

When Johnson became President after Lincoln's assassination, Eliza was ill. She remained in her rooms, hidden from the public.

Julia Dent Grant

1826–1902

Born: St. Louis, Missouri
Married: Ulysses S. Grant, 1848
Children: Fred, Buck, Jesse, Nellie
First Lady: 1869–1877

Julia Grant was thrilled to become First Lady. Now she could spend money lavishly, plan large parties and elaborate twenty-course dinners. She loved hobnobbing with the very rich, and she acted as though she knew no other kind of life.

Her grandest social event was the White House wedding of her daughter, Nellie. One hundred and fifty guests saw the bride march down the aisle in a $5,000 gown. The expense was worthwhile, for the newlyweds received gifts valued at over $75,000.

The woman who now spent money so freely had once doubted that her husband would be able to earn a living for her and their four children. Before he became a famous Civil War general, Grant had failed in every job he undertook. A few years after they were married Ulysses was forced to leave the Army because he drank too much. He tried life as a farmer, but couldn't earn a living. He peddled firewood in the streets of St. Louis. He clerked unsuccessfully in his father's leather-goods store.

When the Civil War broke out Grant volunteered for the Army and finally found success. He advanced until he became commander in chief, the hero of the war. As the wife of a hero, Julia enjoyed a popularity she could never have earned otherwise, for she was quite ordinary. The Presidency was the highest reward the country could give its conquering hero.

When Grant's term of office ended, he and Julia toured the world for two years. Kings and princes entertained them and gave them gifts. After their travels they settled in New York, where rich friends collected money so that the Grants could live in a Fifth Avenue mansion. How different from the life she had led as a peddler's wife!

Lucy Ware Webb Hayes

1831–1889

Born: Chillicothe, Ohio
Married: Rutherford B. Hayes, 1852
Children: Birchard, James, Rutherford,
Fanny, Joseph, George, Scott, Manning
First Lady: 1877–1881

In contrast to Julia Grant, Lucy Hayes was a serious-minded woman more interested in social reform than in parties. Instead of elaborate, expensive gowns, Lucy wore simple, high-necked dresses and no jewelry. Instead of elaborate state dinners she arranged informal receptions where guests could stroll about as they chatted. The White House welcomed visitors almost every evening between eight and ten.

Because she refused to serve liquor, the First Lady was nick-named "Lemonade Lucy." Despite her strait-laced ways, she was well liked and the newspapers praised her. An admirer declared that Lucy represented "the new woman era," for she spoke her mind. Interested in better schooling for all and the women's right to vote, she also voiced concern for the poor and the sick.

Lucy's father, an Ohio doctor, died when she was two years old. Her mother arranged that Lucy take courses at the all-male Ohio Wesleyan University. Then Lucy attended Wesleyan Female College in Cincinnati. She was the first President's wife with a college diploma.

When the Civil War broke out, Lucy stated that her only regret was that she could not fight "with a garrison of women." While her husband fought for the Union, she cared for the wounded near battlefields and in hospitals.

During the 1880s, women joined together to protest poverty, prison conditions, and poor schooling. After Lucy left the White House, she continued to be one of the "new women" interested in reform.

Lucretia Rudolph Garfield

1832–1918

Born: Hiram, Ohio
Married: James Garfield, 1858
Children: Eliza, Harry, James,
Mary, Irvin, Abram, Edward
First Lady: 1881

Like Lucy Hayes, Lucretia Garfield was a college graduate. She met her husband when they were both students at Hiram College, Ohio. They were schoolteachers when they were married in 1858.

Lucretia was First Lady for only a few months. She moved into the White House in March 1881. In May she fell ill with malaria, common in Washington, a city then filled with swamps.

Sent to a New Jersey resort to recover, she was there when Garfield was shot on July 2. She returned to the White House and stayed near him until he died of his wounds September 19, 1881.

Ellen Lewis Herndon Arthur

1837–1880

Born: Fredericksburg, Virginia
Married: Chester A. Arthur, 1859
Children: Chester, Jr., Nellie, William

Ellen Arthur died almost ten months before her husband became President. She was from Virginia, not interested in politics, but very active in social life. Washington society would have approved.

Once again, as in Jackson's time, the White House was a house of mourning. President Arthur planned his own dinners and receptions. He felt no one could replace Ellen as his hostess, although occasionally his sister, Mary, helped out. President Arthur managed the household. He arranged to have twenty-four wagonloads of furniture and knick-knacks auctioned off. Then, using elegant taste, he had the White House redecorated.

Frances Folsom Cleveland

1864–1947

Born: Buffalo, New York
Married: Grover Cleveland, 1886
Children: Ruth, Esther, Marion, Francis, Richard
First Lady: 1886–1889; 1893–1897

Although President Grover Cleveland was forty-eight years old, he had never married. Washington hummed with talk about suitable wives for him. One rumor had it that Cleveland was interested in Mrs. Oscar Folsom, the widow of his former law partner. He was not interested in the widow; he was in love with her daughter, Frances Folsom.

Frances' father had been thrown from a carriage and killed when she was eleven years old. Cleveland became her guardian. His fatherly interest changed to a romantic one when Frances was a student at Wells College. Cleveland wrote often, and kept sending her roses.

Despite the twenty-seven years' difference in age, Frances married her "Uncle Cleve." She was almost twenty-two; he was forty-nine. He was the first President to be married in the White House.

The wedding was small and dignified. Church bells rang, naval cannons boomed a twenty-one-gun salute, and the forty guests drank to the newlyweds—with mineral water. Frances did not approve of liquor.

When the newlyweds left for a honeymoon in Maryland they found reporters waiting for them. Some newspapermen were equipped with spy glasses!

The twenty-two-year-old First Lady lost her privacy, but gained fame. The country adored reading about her. She was gorgeous, had a sparkling smile, and always dressed in the height of fashion. At her first afternoon reception women crashed into furniture as they jammed into the White House to see her. On another occasion, 9,000 people queued up just to shake her hand. Several times people hid themselves behind bushes and jumped out to greet her.

Cleveland ran for a second term in 1888, but lost the election. When she moved out of the White House, Frances told the staff, "We are coming back just four years from today"—and they did. They returned in 1893 for another four years.

Caroline Lavinia Scott Harrison

1832–1892

Born: Oxford, Ohio
Married: Benjamin Harrison, 1853
Children: Russell, Mary
First Lady: 1889–1892

A middle-aged woman not interested in fashion was quite a contrast to the young and beautiful Frances Cleveland. Caroline Harrison's plain, easy manner made her more popular than her husband. President Harrison was so stiff and formal he was called a "human iceberg." Caroline provided some human warmth.

Caroline modernized the White House by having electric lights installed. For a long time the Harrisons were afraid of receiving electric shocks, and they wouldn't touch the light switches. They slept with lights blazing throughout the house whenever an electrician failed to switch them off.

The First Lady became ill and died the third year she was in the White House.

Ida Saxton McKinley

1847–1907

Born: Canton, Ohio, 1847
Married: William McKinley, 1871
Children: Katie, Ida
First Lady: 1897–1901

Aged by sorrow, self-pity, and crippling epilepsy, Ida McKinley was hardly able to take on the duties of First Lady.

After four years of marriage, Ida suffered a nervous breakdown following the death of two baby daughters. She never recovered. Fainting spells, depressions, headaches, and epileptic fits were frequent. Ida's sickness was never discussed. It was one of Washington's best-kept secrets. Today, medicine would have controlled her illness.

On September 6, 1901, President McKinley was shot. As he lay dying he was concerned about Ida. "My wife," he said, "be careful how you tell her—oh be careful!"

Edith Kermit Carow Roosevelt

1861–1948

Born: Norwich, Connecticut
Married: Theodore Roosevelt, 1886
Children: Theodore, Jr., Kermit, Ethel, Archibald,
Quentin, and Alice (daughter of first Mrs. Roosevelt)
First Lady: 1901–1909

Edith Roosevelt was an elegant, quiet woman in charge of the most unruly, fun-loving family that ever occupied the White House. President Roosevelt, who enjoyed wrestling with his children, used to let off steam by running out the back door and racing around the Washington Monument. Six noisy children added to the household merriment. No one in history had ever walked up the White House stairs on stilts until the Roosevelt kids came. Nor had a horse ever entered the mansion until young Quentin led a pony into the elevator and into his brother's room.

Coming from one of New York City's rich society families, Edith had been groomed to be a gracious hostess. Teddy's family was also socially prominent. Their life together was a rip-roaring success.

Helen (Nellie) Herron Taft

1861–1943

Born: Cincinnati, Ohio
Married: William Howard Taft, 1886
Children: Helen, Robert, Charles
First Lady: 1909–1913

When President Taft rode to the White House after his inauguration, his First Lady was seated beside him in the carriage. No other President's wife had ever done that before. But Nellie Taft felt she deserved the honor, for she had helped make him President.

Taft wanted to be a judge, not a President. He ran for the highest office because his wife insisted upon it. She knew how to push her weight around, and she used it to push her 350-pound husband in the direction she wanted him to go.

In 1900, President McKinley appointed Will Governor of the Philippines. The Taft family sailed away to Manila, where Nellie enjoyed her role as First Lady of the Philippines.

Four years later, President Roosevelt asked Taft to become Secretary of War. Will preferred to stay in the Philippines but

Nellie would not hear of it, and made him accept. Secretary of War was the "kind of career I wanted for him and expected him to have," she wrote.

The following year President Roosevelt offered to appoint him to the United States Supreme Court. Taft was delighted. This had been his life's ambition. But Nellie made him refuse. "I want you in line for the presidential nomination," she said.

Nellie Taft wasn't able to enjoy being First Lady. A few months after she entered the White House she suffered a stroke. However, a year later she was well enough to sit in on presidential conferences. She looked forward to another term as First Lady.

When Taft failed to be re-elected, Nellie was so upset she didn't say good-bye to the White House staff. (Taft wasn't sorry to leave. Eight years later his dream came true: he became Chief Justice of the United States.)

Nellie Taft is best remembered today, not for her influence on a President, but because of the three thousand cherry trees she had shipped from Japan to Washington.

Ellen Louise Axson Wilson

1860–1914

Born: Savannah, Georgia
Married: Woodrow Wilson, 1885
Children: Margaret, Eleanor, Jessie
First Lady: 1913–1914

"The White House has no attractions for me," Ellen Wilson wrote. She was a brilliant, well-read woman, happiest when her husband was a professor of history at Bryn Mawr College.

When Ellen Wilson came to Washington she was more interested in social conditions than in giving parties. When she took some congressmen through Washington's crowded black slums they were so shocked they passed a slum clearance bill.

Ellen Wilson was First Lady for only a year and a half. She died in the White House in August 1914.

Edith Bolling Galt Wilson

1872–1961

Born: Wytheville, Virginia
Married: Norman Galt, 1896; widowed 1908
Children: None

Married: Woodrow Wilson, 1915
Children: None
First Lady: 1915–1921

A year and four months after his first wife's death, President Wilson married Edith Galt, the widow of a Washington jeweler. She became Wilson's chief adviser. He told her everything. During World War I only Edith was allowed to know the President's secret code for sending messages to Europe. Wilson wrote them himself and Edith translated them into code, a task she undertook for four and a half years. She attended all his conferences. When Wilson sailed for Europe for the peace conference, she went along. Because no women were allowed, President Wilson arranged for her to stay in a small anteroom hidden by heavy red curtains. She confessed she was "hot but happy."

On September 25, 1919, President Wilson suffered a paralytic stroke. As her husband lay helplessly in bed, Edith took over as unofficial acting President. There seemed to be no other choice. Vice President Marshall, a pleasant fellow, confessed that he wasn't capable of running the country. Wilson's doctor advised Edith that, for her husband's sake, she should not let him resign, but she should carry on.

Edith Wilson was unofficial acting President for at least four months. Some historians believe she was acting President seventeen months, until the end of Wilson's term. It's difficult to decide, because she hid her role. She knew the country would be in a fury if they knew a woman was head of the government. When she made decisions, she pretended that they came from her sick husband. Every important document went to her. She worked days and nights. If her husband was well enough, she asked his opinon; when he was too ill, she made all the decisions herself. Sometimes she guided his hand as he signed congressional bills.

Although the general public didn't know what was going on, Congress was upset. One senator roared, "We have a petticoat government! Mrs. Wilson is President!" Some called her "Mrs. President"; others, "The Presidentress of the United States."

Wilson recovered and, under her guidance, completed his term.

How strange that the woman who acted as President was against equal rights for women. She opposed their right to vote. Perhaps, having once been a southern belle, she felt any political interest was not "feminine."

Florence Kling Harding

1860–1924

Born: Marion, Ohio
Married: Henry de Wolfe, 1880; divorced 1886
Children: Eugene

Married: Warren G. Harding, 1891
Children: None
First Lady: 1921–1923

The American public was happy to welcome a First Lady who described herself and her husband as "just plain folks." After the secrecy of the Wilson years, what a good feeling it was to see the White House gates unlocked. Florence Harding was so friendly she often came down to the first floor to greet tourists. She shook hands with thousands, and was a marvelous hostess at big receptions and gorgeous garden parties.

What the public didn't know was that Florence was on hand to serve liquor for the President and his "Ohio gang," hometown friends, some of them vulgar and dishonest. The Hardings ignored the prohibition law, which barred liquor. Florence enjoyed being bartender while Warren and his buddies played cards until the early hours of the morning. The gang enjoyed having her around. They called the First Lady "Duchess."

Florence Harding boasted she always knew "what was best for Warren." She was one of his chief advisers. Sometimes, when he had to reach a decision, Warren would say, "I'll have to check with the Duchess." She helped him run the country downhill, advising him on federal appointments, sitting in on important conferences.

Florence was the daughter of the richest banker in Marion, Ohio. When she met Warren she had been divorced.

This strong-willed woman pushed Warren Harding up the political ladder. In 1914, when Harding was elected senator from Ohio, they moved to Washington. Encouraged by Ohio's political boss, Harry Daugherty, Florence insisted that he run for President. He didn't want to be President, but she wanted to be First Lady.

After he won the election Florence called herself a "President-maker" and a "President-ruler." Her husband moaned, "I have lost my freedom."

In 1923 Harding died suddenly of a blood clot. After his death, scandals were uncovered about his crooked administration. Florence burned the President's papers before she died a year later.

Grace Anna Goodhue Coolidge

1879–1957

Born: Burlington, Vermont
Married: Calvin Coolidge, 1905
Children: John, Calvin, Jr.
First Lady: 1923–1929

When President Harding died, a messenger had to be sent to notify Vice President Coolidge and his wife, because they didn't own a private telephone.

Grace Coolidge was timid about becoming First Lady. She was accustomed to a quiet life in a two-family house that didn't even have electricity. She always did her own cooking and cleaning. However, she became such a marvelous hostess that some reporters compared her with Dolley Madison. General Pershing, Queen Marie of Rumania, Will Rogers, the composer Rachmaninoff were among the many famous people who enjoyed her hospitality. She was witty and attractive. Added to that, she was a baseball fan, which made her an All-American First Lady.

Called a "champion smiler," she kept conversations going. That was important for the wife of "silent Cal." He so rarely talked, someone said that whenever he opened his mouth a moth flew out.

The President had other peculiar ways. He went over all the household bills, and kept Grace on a strict budget. He didn't talk to her about government matters. Grace claimed she knew only what she read in the newspapers or heard on the radio.

Coolidge did not want his wife to talk to the press. At a luncheon for newspaper women, Grace was asked to say a few words. She did not open her mouth. However, she made a five-minute speech, using sign language she had learned when she taught the deaf.

Grace was the daughter of a Burlington, Vermont, ship inspector. After graduating from the University of Vermont, she spent four years teaching at the Clarke School for the Deaf in Northhampton, Massachusetts. Calvin Coolidge, a local lawyer, claims he won Grace because he "outsat everybody else."

Their sixteen-year-old son, Calvin, Jr., died of blood poisoning eleven months after they entered the White House.

In 1927 Coolidge surprised the nation and Grace by stating, "I do not choose to run for President in 1928." No long speech from "silent Cal."

Lou Henry Hoover

1874–1944

Born: Waterloo, Iowa
Married: Herbert Clark Hoover, 1899
Children: Herbert, Jr., Allan
First Lady: 1929–1933

As a young woman Lou Hoover loved hiking, camping, and geology, the study of rocks. She was the only girl in the geology class at Stanford University. Her brilliance and charm impressed Herbert Hoover, another geology student.

The day after their wedding, they sailed to the Orient for Hoover's job as Director of Mines for China. Lou went on field trips with him, traveling by canal boat, pack mule, and oxcart. Sometimes they rode ponies along dangerous roads, while guards galloped ahead to protect them against bandits. Lou kept house in shacks and tents. To enjoy her adventures more fully, she learned to speak Chinese.

The Hoovers were trapped in the city of Tsientsin during the Boxer Uprising, a peasant war against all "foreign devils." Lou rode her bike through gunfire, going from house to house to gather bandages for the wounded. One time her bicycle was hit by a bullet. Another time a bullet entered her house and whizzed over her head.

After China, using London and Palo Alto, California, as headquarters, the Hoovers lived in Ceylon, Malaysia, Japan, Burma, and Siberia.

During this time Lou translated a sixteenth-century Latin book on metals into English. Her book is still being used by scientists.

As First Lady, Lou Hoover exchanged a life of adventure for a quiet term in the White House. She shied away from publicity, except when she wanted to tell about her pet project, the Girl Scouts. She was its national president at one time. Lou restored historic rooms in the White House at her own expense, and she added her own money in order to entertain lavishly. The Hoovers were millionaires.

The stock market crash of 1929 and the country's worst depression cast a shadow over her years as First Lady. She was upset to learn that the unemployed called their shack towns "Hoovervilles," and shocked when her husband lost so badly in the election of 1932.

Anna Eleanor Roosevelt Roosevelt

1884–1962

Born: New York City
Married: Franklin Delano Roosevelt, 1905
Children: Anna, James, Franklin (died as infant),
Elliott, Franklin, Jr., John
First Lady: 1933–1945

A shy, homely girl, the ugly duckling of her family, became one of the world's most admired women.

Eleanor Roosevelt's parents died when she was a child. Relatives wondered whether anyone would ever want to marry her. How surprised they were when Franklin Delano Roosevelt, a startlingly handsome fifth cousin, fell in love with her and married her.

Her husband's career nearly ended in the summer of 1921, when he was crippled by polio. Eleanor stubbornly refused to allow her husband to lead the life of a helpless, sheltered cripple. With the backing of Franklin's close friend Louis Howe, she convinced him to stay in politics. By 1929 he was governor of New York. And by 1933 he was President.

He was the first President to admit his wife's strong influence. "Eleanor and I" was an expression the men in Washington had to get used to.

As First Lady she was resented by some, laughed at by many, and loved by millions. There never was anyone quite like her. She visited mines, prisons, hospitals, slums. During World War II, she flew to army camps all over the world.

Independent, rejecting the pampered role usually played by First Ladies, Eleanor ran the White House elevator herself and drove her own car. No chauffeur or Secret Service agents for her! She walked, took trains, and flew on commercial air flights.

Eleanor wrote "My Day," a newspaper column that expressed her ideas. She also gave lectures and radio broadcasts. Best of all, she pressed reforms in Washington, aware that human misery could be lessened if Congress acted.

In 1945 President Roosevelt died suddenly. Instead of retiring, she started the most important career of her life as United Nations Chairman of the Commission on Human Rights. The shy, homely child had become "First Lady of the World."

Elizabeth Virginia Wallace Truman

1885–

Born: Independence, Missouri
Married: Harry S Truman, 1919
Children: Margaret
First Lady: 1945–1953

Newspapers and radio commentators described Bess Truman as a plain, ordinary housewife from Independence, Missouri. She never bothered to change that image. Bess preferred her privacy to the limelight, and would rather say she was a "nobody" than talk about herself at interviews.

There was nothing ordinary about Bess. President Truman called her "my chief adviser." He never made a speech without first showing her the text. He consulted her on every major decision—even about using the atom bomb and entering the Korean War. Truman made up his own mind, but first he asked his wife's opinion. He called her "a full partner in all my transactions—politically and otherwise."

Harry enjoyed introducing her as "the boss," or "the boss who bosses the boss." Bess made no comment.

Bess was a hard-working First Lady. Although the White House staff could have planned social events, Bess did the job herself. Harry was so proud of her ability to be a kind, gracious hostess, he said, "She made sure that snooty women were well treated. That's something I wouldn't do . . . I wouldn't talk to them."

Being in the White House didn't change Bess Truman. She still ran her life as though she were back in Missouri, phoning old friends, enjoying their visits, playing Ping-Pong with her daughter, Margaret. When she visited her hometown, she did her own cooking and shopping.

Truman confessed he fell for Bess at Sunday school, when he was six and she was five. They graduated together from Independence High School. A popular, attractive, athletic girl, Bess was in no hurry to marry, but she finally did when Harry returned from service in World War I.

When her husband became senator they moved to a modest five-room apartment in Washington. Bess worked as Harry's secretary. Even when he was Vice President, the Trumans continued to live in the same small apartment.

When Bess Truman returned to Independence, neighbors felt she had never left. Bess was the same as ever. The White House years didn't spoil her.

Mamie Geneva Doud Eisenhower

1896–1979

Born: Boone, Iowa
Married: Dwight David Eisenhower, 1916
Children: Doud Dwight, John Sheldon
First Lady: 1953–1961

"What American woman wouldn't want her husband to be President?" Mamie asked. Mamie was listed among the world's most admired women in newspaper polls. The country loved her.

Being First Lady meant, for Mamie, being White House hostess, nothing more. She was never interested in politics; she had no special hobbies. She relaxed by playing cards, and by being with her family.

She was eighteen years old when she met Ike, an army lieutenant, "the spiffiest looking man I ever talked to in all my born life." They were married the following year.

The Eisenhowers had twenty-seven homes in thirty-eight years, at army posts all over the world. Their greatest sorrow was the death of a three-year-old son, Doud Dwight, from scarlet fever. A second son, John Sheldon, born a year and a half after the tragedy, made a career in the Army. John's son David married former President Nixon's daughter Julie.

During World War II, while Ike was commander in chief in Europe, Mamie lived in a Washington apartment. After the war, the Eisenhowers bought a farm in Gettysburg, Pennsylvania. It was the first home they ever owned.

Before he was elected President, Ike headed NATO (North Atlantic Treaty Organization). He and Mamie lived in a palace near Paris, and they were entertained by royalty all over Europe.

Eisenhower won the presidential election as America's war hero, and Mamie was loved as a hero's wife.

Jacqueline Lee Bouvier Kennedy

1929–

Born: Southhampton, New York
Married: John Fitzgerald Kennedy, 1953
Children: Caroline, John, Jr., Patrick (died in infancy)
First Lady: 1961–1963

Because Jacqueline Kennedy was such a beautiful, bright, charming First Lady, the world wanted to know everything about her. She was America's dream girl, and the press wrote about her the way they do about glamorous Hollywood stars.

She was a photographer's dream, for she skied, swam, rode horseback like a champion, and dressed with style and taste. She became a fashion-setter. The "Jackie look" was the look women everywhere wanted. They saw it in fashion magazines, in stores, and on their children's dolls.

Jackie came from a socially prominent family. After studying at Vassar and the Sorbonne in Paris, she worked as "The Inquiring Camera Girl" for the Washington *Times-Herald*. Friends introduced her to Jack Kennedy, the handsome senator from Massachusetts.

Although Jackie had no interest in politics, as First Lady she became one of our best unofficial ambassadors. Venezuelan peasants shouted their approval after she addressed them in Spanish. Her beauty and ability to speak French created such a sensation in Paris that President Kennedy introduced himself as "the man who accompanied Jackie Kennedy." When she toured India and Pakistan, crowds clamored to see the "Queen of America," and when she visited Ottawa, a reporter wrote, "Jackie Kennedy captured the Canadian capital without firing a shot."

According to Jackie, her most important achievement as First Lady was refurnishing the White House. Using pieces that had been hidden in storerooms for ages, and buying furniture that belonged to former Presidents, she gave the White House a "new look." Jackie proved to be a first-rate commentator when she guided millions of Americans on a television tour of the White House. Without using a script, she talked about the history and beauty of every room.

When President Kennedy was shot in Dallas, he slumped into his wife's arms. The world will never forget the pathetic figure of a widow and two children standing beside President Kennedy's coffin.

Claudia Taylor (Lady Bird) Johnson

1912–

Born: Karnack, Texas
Married: Lyndon B. Johnson, 1934
Children: Lynda Bird, Luci Baines
First Lady: 1963–1969

Two First Ladies were Johnsons. Both were Southerners, and each came to the White House after a President was assassinated. The worldly, wealthy Lady Bird was quite a contrast to Eliza Johnson, the plain woman from a Tennessee shack.

Lady Bird was born in a country mansion near Karnack, Texas. (She was nicknamed by a nursemaid who said she was "purty as a ladybird.") Her mother died when she was five years old. Brought up by an aunt and family servants, Lady Bird went to a one-room school until she was thirteen. Then her father bought her a car so she could drive herself to high school fourteen miles away. Lady Bird graduated from the University of Texas before she married Johnson.

While Johnson was busy with politics, Lady Bird was interested in business. Using money she had inherited from her mother, she

(53)

bought a small Texas radio station. Under her management the station made millions.

When Johnson was Vice President, the family lived in a magnificent mansion in Washington and at the enormous LBJ Ranch in Texas. Although Lady Bird staged large, beautiful parties in Washington, she preferred to entertain in Texas. Senators, United Nations' delegates, astronauts, and an Asian camel driver were among the many who enjoyed her southern hospitality.

Lady Bird had planned a barbecue for President Kennedy the day he was shot in Dallas. The Johnsons were in the same motorcade on that fateful day, and within hours they were rushed to Washington.

Lady Bird played an active role during Johnson's term. Visiting slums and mines, she reported conditions to her husband Eleanor Roosevelt-style. She crisscrossed the country lecturing for her own pet project, making America more beautiful. The President said, "I listen to her more than to any person I know." He said he took her advice when he decided not to run in 1968.

Thelma Catherine (Patricia) Ryan Nixon

1912–

Born: Ely, Nevada
Married: Richard Milhous Nixon, 1940
Children: Tricia, Julie
First Lady: 1969–1974

Pat's father was a poor Nevada miner who, hoping to earn a better living, moved his family to a California farm. Pat's mother died when she was thirteen years old, and her father died when she was seventeen. Pat managed to finish high school and go to the University of Southern California. She supported herself working as a sales clerk and as a movie "extra."

After college Pat taught typing at Whittier High School. She joined an amateur theater group, where she met Richard Nixon, an ambitious lawyer. He won the role of district attorney—in a play. He also won Pat's heart.

A few years after they were married Nixon became active in politics. He started his career as congressman; six years later he was Vice President under Eisenhower. Pat had mixed feelings about her role. She claimed this wasn't the life she would have chosen for herself. Although she enjoyed traveling all over the world with Nixon, she wanted more time to be home with her daughters, Tricia and Julie. Twice she had her husband promise in writing that he would quit politics. But Richard Nixon couldn't stop.

Big parades, elaborate receptions, and six inaugural balls welcomed President and Mrs. Nixon in 1969. Over $4 million was spent celebrating. The First Lady became part of an enormous organization running the White House. She was hostess at affairs planned and produced by a large staff. Pat played a more important role as "Personal Representative of the President." Nixon sent her on goodwill tours to Africa and South America.

Pat and her daughters were distressed whenever anyone criticized the President. She suffered agony when Nixon resigned.

Elizabeth Bloomer Ford

1918–

Born: Chicago, Illinois
Married: William Warren, 1942; divorced 1947
Children: None

Married: Gerald R. Ford, 1948
Children: Michael, John, Steven, Susan
First Lady: 1974–1977

Unlike Presidents' wives before her, Betty Ford became First Lady without her husband campaigning to be Vice President or President. Gerald Ford had never run for any office higher than congressman, and he seemed happy to remain a congressman.

What a surprise when President Nixon chose him to be Vice President after Vice President Agnew resigned. Then the final shock came in August, 1974: President Nixon resigned. Ford became President and Betty was First Lady.

For the first time in her married life Betty didn't have to cook or clean house. Gorgeously gowned, she was in her glory dining with kings and queens and prime ministers.

This was a far cry from Betty Bloomer, the salesman's daughter, who grew up in Grand Rapids, Michigan. She wanted to be a professional dancer. Betty worked in New York City as a photographer's model to pay for dance lessons, and for a short time she was a member of the Martha Graham Dance Troupe.

When Gerald Ford met Betty she was in Grand Rapids, working in a department store. A few weeks after they married he was elected congressman.

As a congressman's wife, Betty didn't voice her opinions openly. But as First Lady, Betty spoke out on issues that shocked some and delighted others. "Being ladylike does not require silence," she said. "I do not believe being First Lady should prevent me from expressing my ideas." At times she openly disagreed with her husband about his political appointments. He agreed with her about women's rights, but Betty spoke louder and stronger about it than he.

Television's magic window enabled the public to see an attractive, spirited woman and her appealing family.

"Vote for Betty's Husband" was printed on 1976 campaign buttons. Sometimes she rated higher than the President in popularity polls.

Rosalynn Smith Carter

1927–

Born: Plains, Georgia
Married: James Earl Carter, 1946
Children: Jack, James (Chip), Jeffrey, Amy
First Lady: 1977–1981

Her father was a garage mechanic who died when Rosalynn was only thirteen. Her mother supported four children by sewing for other people and working at the post office. Rosalynn helped out when she was fifteen, working in a Plains, Georgia, beauty parlor. "We were very, very poor, and we worked very hard," she recalls.

Rosalynn's family and the Carter family had been close ever since Jimmy's mother helped take care of Rosalynn's sick father. Rosalynn married Jimmy after she graduated from Georgia Southwestern Junior College and he graduated from the U.S. Naval Academy.

The President says his wife has always been his "equal partner" in business and in politics. Rosalynn kept the books for the Carter peanut business. She attended political conferences and was out front campaigning for Jimmy's successful races for senator and governor of Georgia.

Rosalynn was a champion campaigner in 1976. Working sixteen hours a day, five days a week, she showed up at factories at four in the morning, at church gatherings and shopping centers during the day, and at dinners and rallies at night. She talked seriously during press conferences about subjects important to the country.

Rosalynn helped Jimmy decide to run for President, and she helped him win.

Anne Frances (Nancy) Robbins Davis Reagan

1923–

Born: New York City
Married: Ronald Wilson Reagan, 1952
Children: Patricia Ann, Ronald Prescott
(Maureen, Michael: two children of Ronald Reagan's
by a former marriage)
First Lady: 1981–

Nancy Reagan has often said that her life really began when she married the man she loved. She is so happy being a full-time wife and mother that she has never regretted giving up her career as an actress. Nancy is a former movie star who appeared in eleven Hollywood films.

When she married actor Ronald Reagan she never dreamed that he would be governor of California and she would be its First Lady for eight years. Nor could she ever have imagined that her husband would become President and she would be First Lady of the United States.

Born Anne Frances Robbins, her last name was changed to Davis after her divorced mother remarried and her stepfather, Dr. Loyal Davis, adopted her.

Nancy graduated from Smith College, in Northampton, Massachusetts. During World War II she was a nurse's aide and a salesperson in a department store. Nancy began her acting career by accepting small parts in plays of stock companies that toured the country. Before moving to Hollywood and becoming one of its hopeful young actresses, she played minor roles on Broadway and in television shows.

Nancy doesn't intend to be active in government affairs. She claims that she will not try to shape the President's policies. Charming, clever, and elegant, she plays the most important role of her life, always in the limelight at the White House.

Bibliography

Barzman, Sol	*The First Ladies*	Cowles Book Co., 1970
Bassett, Margaret	*Profiles and Portraits of American Presidents*	Bond, Wheelwright, Co., Freeport, Maine, 1969
Butterfield, Roger	*The American Past*	Simon and Schuster, 1947
Durant, Alice and John	*The Presidents*	A. A. Gache & Son, Miami, Florida, 1955
Flexner, Jane	*Washington*	Little Brown, 1969
Furman, Bess	*White House Profile*	Bobbs Merrill, 1951
Hagedorn, Hermann	*The Roosevelt Family of Sagamore Hill*	Macmillan, 1954
James, Edward T. and Janet W., eds.	*Notable American Women, 1607–1950: A Biographical Dictionary*	Belknap Press, 1971
Klapthor, Margaret	*The First Ladies*	White House Historical Association, 1975
Lash, Joseph	*Eleanor and Franklin*	New American Library, 1971
McConnell, Jane and Burt	*Our First Ladies*	Crowell Co., 1969
Means, Marianne	*The Woman in the White House*	Random House, 1963
Miller, Merle	*Plain Speaking*	Berkley Publishing, paperback, 1973
Montgomery, Ruth	*Mrs. LBJ*	Holt, Rinehart & Winston, 1964
Pryer, Helen	*Lou Henry Hoover*	Dodd Mead & Co., 1969
Remini, Robert	*Andrew Jackson*	Twayne Publishers, 1969
Simons, Dawn	*A Rose for Mrs. Lincoln*	Beacon Press, Boston, 1970
Thane, Elswyth	*Washington's Lady*	Duell Sloane & Pearce, 1954
Vestal, Bud	*Jerry Ford Up Close*	Coward McCann Geoghegan, 1974
Wallechinsky, David and Wallace, Irving	*The People's Almanac*	Doubleday, 1975

Index

About the Author

Rhoda Blumberg has had a varied writing career. She has written for radio talk shows, authored many magazine articles on a variety of subjects, written almost a dozen travel guides, and has had three First Books published by Franklin Watts: *Fire Fighters, Sharks* and *UFO.* The desire to write this book, *First Ladies,* grew out of her realization that little has been written about the contributions and personalities of these very important women in American history.